MEATMEN
COOKING CHANNEL

HAWKER FAVOURITES
POPULAR SINGAPOREAN STREET FOODS

mc Marshall Cavendish
Cuisine

© 2016 Marshall Cavendish International (Asia) Private Limited

Photographer: Tan Junjie
Editor: Lydia Leong
Designer: Bernard Go Kwang Meng

Published by Marshall Cavendish Cuisine
An imprint of Marshall Cavendish International

Other Marshall Cavendish Offices:
Marshall Cavendish Corporation. 99 White Plains Road, Tarrytown NY
10591-9001, USA • Marshall Cavendish International (Thailand) Co Ltd.
253 Asoke, 12th Flr, Sukhumvit 21 Road, Klongtoey Nua, Wattana,
Bangkok 10110, Thailand • Marshall Cavendish (Malaysia) Sdn Bhd,
Times Subang, Lot 46, Subang Hi-Tech Industrial Park, Batu Tiga,
40000 Shah Alam, Selangor Darul Ehsan, Malaysia.

Marshall Cavendish is a trademark of Times Publishing Limited

National Library Board, Singapore Cataloguing-in-Publication Data

Name(s): MeatMen Cooking Channel.
Title: MeatMen Cooking Channel hawker favourites : popular Singaporean street
foods / Meatmen.
Description: Singapore : Marshall Cavendish Cuisine, [2016]
Identifier(s): OCN 953741618 | ISBN 978-981-47-5163-6 (hardcover)
Subject(s): LCSH: Cooking, Singaporean. | Street food--Singapore. | Cookbooks.
Classification: DDC 641.595957--dc23

Printed by Times Offset (M) Sdn Bhd

DEDICATION

This book is dedicated to the hawkers of Asia, for the blood, sweat and long hours spent honing their craft every single day.

We would also like to dedicate this book to our fans on social media and beyond, for their support and encouragement since 2013.

CONTENTS

ACKNOWLEDGEMENTS

The completion of this recipe book would not have been possible without the support of many people. We're sincerely appreciative and grateful for the support we've received so far. Specifically, we'd like to acknowledge the following folks:

Lydia and Mindy and the team from Marshall Cavendish International (Asia) for their constant support in pursuing this book.

The families of our team for their understanding despite the countless hours we poured into this passion, simplifying local Asian recipes for the benefit of food lovers.

Thank you all.

The MeatMen Cooking Channel

INTRODUCTION

Hawker dishes are definitely a staple food in Singapore. It's what we talk about among our family and friends and even with complete strangers! We debate about where to find the best Hokkien mee and argue about which chicken rice stall has the longest queue, but despite this, not many of us know how to prepare these dishes for ourselves. Some also think that it takes too much work to cook something that can be easily found at any hawker centre.

This was when we realised how important it was for us to document the recipes and share how these hawker favourites can be recreated without too much fuss right at home. You won't need fancy tools or an elaborate set-up to prepare these dishes as we have carefully researched and tweaked the recipes so that the dishes can be prepared with whatever tools you have at home whether in Singapore or overseas.

The know-how of doing these dishes and the nostalgic flavours are definitely worth preserving, and we trust that you will enjoy this journey of discovery of the processes and tastes. May these dishes be part of your dining repertoire for many years to come.

ABOUT THE MEATMEN
COOKING CHANNEL

We are simply a bunch of greedy guys in the creative trade who love their food, be it eating, cooking, growing or even capturing it on film.

It all started with the obsession to record the whole process of food creation through the lens. That passion soon spread and before long, we were infected with the food-frenzy craze.

We are about being simple. Our vision is simple, to prove that cooking at home is not difficult. We hope to simplify it for everyone to make cooking easy and fun for all.

The MeatMen Cooking Channel symbolises a vision we have to bring awesome local dish dishes from hawker centres and coffee shops to the comfort of our own homes.

Chris Lim

Kiat Yingda

Tan Junjie

Jonathan Tan

NOODLES AND RICE

Hokkien mee is popular favourite among the locals in Singapore. We think that the MAGIC of this dish is in the seafood and the pork bone broth. The broth is key in producing the irreplaceable flavour that makes us all love Hokkien mee so much, and we are proud to say that this recipe produces a dish that will give your favourite hawker a run for his money!

HOKKIEN MEE STIR-FRIED PRAWN NOODLES

Serves 4

1.5 kg (4 lb 3½ oz) prawns, rinsed and peeled, heads and shells reserved

200 g (7 oz) pork belly

4 slices ginger

2 medium squid

Pork lard, as needed

4 eggs

600 g (1 lb 5⅓ oz) round yellow noodles

300 g (11 oz) fresh thick *bee hoon* (rice vermicelli)

300 g (11 oz) dried *bee hoon* (rice vermicelli), soaked to soften

2 tsp dark soy sauce

4 tsp light soy sauce

4 Tbsp minced garlic

2 fish cakes, sliced

40 g (1⅓ oz) bean sprouts, trimmed

100 g (3½ oz) Chinese chives, cut into 5-cm (2-in) lengths

Sambal belacan, to taste

4 limes

STOCK

2 Tbsp cooking oil

3 cloves garlic, peeled, sliced

3 shallots, peeled and sliced

2 litres (64 fl oz / 8 cups) boiling water

1 Tbsp white peppercorns

80 g (2⁴/₅ oz) *ikan bilis* (dried anchovies), rinsed

30 g (1 oz) rock sugar

1 Tbsp fish sauce

1 kg (2 lb 3 oz) pork bones, rinsed

1. Rinse and peel prawns. Set prawns aside. Reserve shells and heads for use in stock.

2. Prepare stock. Heat in a large pot over medium heat. Add garlic and shallots and stir-fry until fragrant.

3. Add prawn heads and shells and stir-fry until fragrant.

4. Add boiling water, peppercorns, *ikan bilis*, rock sugar, fish sauce and pork bones. Bring to a boil, then lower heat and let simmer for 45 minutes.

5. In the meantime, blanch pork belly in a pot of boiling water with ginger. Drain and slice into small strips. Set aside.

6. Clean squid and slice. Set aside.

7. Strain stock and return to a boil. Lightly blanch squid, then prawns, in stock.

8. Stir-fry each portion of Hokkien noodles separately. Heat 2 Tbsp pork lard in a hot wok. Add a beaten egg and stir-fry quickly.

9. Add a quarter each of the yellow noodles, thick *bee hoon* and thin *bee hoon* and stir-fry again quickly to mix. Add a little dark soy sauce for colour.

10. Push noodles to one side of wok. One other side of wok, add 1 tsp light soy sauce and stir-fry 1 Tbsp minced garlic with a little more lard.

11. Add a quarter portion of squid, prawns, pork belly and fish cake. Add 125 ml (4 fl oz / ½ cup) stock and a quarter of bean sprouts. Stir-fry with noodles and mix well. Cover wok and leave to cook 3 minutes.

12. Add a little dark soy sauce for colour if needed. Add a handful of chives and stir-fry to mix.

13. Dish out to a serving plate. Repeat to prepare another 3 servings.

14. Serve with *sambal belacan* and cut limes on the side.

Black or white? There's a never-ending debate over which is the
preferred version of carrot cake, and we're happy to say WE DID BOTH.
Who needs to make a choice when you can have both?

CHAI TOW KWAY FRIED CARROT CAKE, BLACK AND WHITE

Serves 2

6 Tbsp pork lard

250 g (9 oz) home-made
or store-bought steamed
carrot cake, cut into 1-cm
($1/2$-in) thick strips

20 g ($2/3$ oz) minced garlic

40 g ($1 1/3$ oz) *chye poh*
(salted radish), rinsed
to get rid of excess salt

1 tsp fish sauce

2 eggs, lightly beaten

2 Tbsp thick sweet sauce,
for black version only

2 Tbsp chopped spring onion
(scallion)

1. Heat 3 Tbsp pork lard in a wok over medium heat.
   Add carrot cake and pan-fry until lightly crisp and
   brown on the sides.

2. Push carrot cake to one side of wok.

3. Add remaining pork lard, minced garlic and *chye poh*
   and stir-fry until fragrant. Mix with carrot cake.

4. Season with fish sauce. Add eggs.

5. To make white version, cook until carrot cake
   is lightly browned on both sides.

6. To make black version, stir-fry to mix eggs with
   carrot cake. Add thick sweet sauce and mix well.
   Ensure that carrot cake is evenly coated.

7. Dish out and garnish with chopped spring onion.

Above: Black Chai Tow Kway
Right: White Chai Tow Kway

This is a fan favourite! The typical Singaporean *char kway teow* consists
of pork lard, *lup cheong*, bean sprouts, eggs and cockles —
ingredients close to our hearts and flavours that we grew up with.

CHAR KWAY TEOW

Serves 2

4 prawns, peeled and
deveined

2 Tbsp pork lard

2 Tbsp minced garlic

200 g (7 oz) flat rice noodles

50 g (1³⁄₄ oz) round yellow
noodles

¹⁄₂ medium fish cake,
thinly sliced

¹⁄₂ *lup cheong* (Chinese
wine sausage), sliced
thinly on the diagonal

1 Tbsp dark soy sauce

2 Tbsp *kecap manis*
(Indonesian sweet soy
sauce)

1 Tbsp sambal chilli (optional)

60 g bean sprouts, trimmed

1 egg, beaten

50 g (1³⁄₄ oz) fresh cockles,
shelled

1. Boil a small pot of water and blanch prawns lightly.
   Drain and set aside.

2. Heat pork lard in a wok over medium heat. Add minced
   garlic and stir-fry until fragrant.

3. Add flat rice noodles and yellow noodles and stir-fry
   until noodles start to soften. Add 2 Tbsp water if
   mixture is dry.

4. Add fish cake and *lup cheong* and stir-fry to mix.

5. Add dark soy sauce and *kecap manis*. Add sambal
   chilli for a slightly spicy dish if desired. Stir-fry until
   noodles are well-coated.

6. Add bean sprouts and egg, and stir-fry for another
   minute.

7. Add cockles and prawns, and stir-fry for another
   20 seconds. Dish out and serve.

At first glance, one might think that *mee soto* is *just* noodles in soup.
That cannot be further from the truth! In Asia, *mee soto* is a hawker hero that can be found
on the menu of almost every food stall for a good reason — it's damn *sedap*!

MEE SOTO CHICKEN NOODLE SOUP

Serves 4

50 g (1³/₄ oz) coriander seeds

10 g (¹/₃ oz) white
    peppercorns

6 cloves garlic

8 candlenuts

40 g (1¹/₃ oz) ginger, peeled
    and sliced

40 g (1¹/₃ oz) galangal, peeled
    and sliced

1 medium red onion, peeled
    and sliced

4 Tbsp cooking oil

20 cardamom pods

5 star anise

10 cloves

1 cinnamon stick

3 litres (96 fl oz / 12 cups)
    packaged chicken stock

3 chicken thighs and legs

3 stalks lemongrass, ends
    trimmed and bruised

1 Tbsp sugar

2 Tbsp salt

800 g (1³/₄ lb) round yellow
    noodles

160 g (5²/₃ oz) bean sprouts,
    trimmed

60 g (2 oz) fried shallots

Chopped coriander leaves
    (cilantro)

1. In a hot dry wok, toast coriander seeds with white peppercorns until fragrant.

2. Place toasted coriander seeds, peppercorns, garlic, candlenuts, ginger, galangal and onion in food processor and blend into a fine paste.

3. Heat oil in a pot over medium heat. Add cardamom pods, star anise, cloves, cinnamon stick and spice paste and stir-fry until fragrant.

4. Add chicken stock, chicken thighs and legs. Add lemongrass and bring to a boil. Lower heat, cover pot and simmer for 45 minutes.

5. Remove chicken from stock and set aside to cool before shredding.

6. Strain stock back into pot. Add sugar and salt. Adjust to taste.

7. Prepare each serving of *mee soto* separately. Blanch a quarter of yellow noodles with a quarter of bean sprouts. Place into a serving bowl.

8. Top with a handful of shredded chicken and add a ladleful of stock. Garnish with fried shallots and coriander leaves.

9. Repeat to prepare another 3 servings. Serve hot.

Bak chor mee is a uniquely Singaporean dish that showcases our love for pork. Honestly, it uses so many parts of the pig, from the different cuts of the meat to the offal. And it all tastes great, especially with the vinegar-braised mushrooms.

BAK CHOR MEE MINCED PORK NOODLES

Serves 4

100 g (3¹/₂ oz) lean pork, thinly sliced

100 g (3¹/₂ oz) pork liver, thinly sliced

200 g (7 oz) minced pork

300 g (11 oz) *mee pok* (flat egg noodles)

8 pork meatballs

60 g (2 oz) bean sprouts, trimmed

4 large lettuce leaves

Fried pork lard

Chopped spring onion (scallion)

MARINADE

Light soy sauce, as needed

Ground white pepper, as needed

Cornflour, as needed

Sesame oil, as needed

MEAT STOCK

2 litres (64 fl oz / 8 cups) water

1 kg (2 lb 3 oz) pork bones, rinsed

80 g (2⁴/₅ oz) *ikan bilis* (dried anchovies)

100 g (3¹/₂ oz) soybeans

¹/₂ Tbsp sugar

1 tsp salt

BRAISED MUSHROOMS

50 g (1³/₄ oz) dried shiitake mushrooms

625 ml (20 fl oz / 2¹/₂ cups) hot water

30 g (1 oz) rock sugar

2 Tbsp dark soy sauce

3 Tbsp light soy sauce

3 Tbsp oyster sauce

1 Tbsp fish sauce

3 Tbsp black vinegar

2 Tbsp sesame oil

NOODLE SAUCE (PER SERVING)

2 Tbsp pork lard

2 tsp light soy sauce

1 tsp black vinegar or to taste

1 tsp fish sauce

1 tsp sambal chilli

3 Tbsp braised mushroom sauce (from braised mushrooms)

1. Soak dried shiitake mushrooms for making braised mushrooms in hot water for 45 minutes.

2. Prepare meat stock. Bring water to the boil in a pot. Add pork bones, *ikan bilis* and soybeans. Lower heat, cover pot and let simmer for 1 hour.

3. Prepare braised mushrooms. Pour mushroom soaking liquid into a slow cooker. Slice soaked mushrooms into strips and add to slow cooker. Add rock sugar, soy sauces, oyster sauce, fish sauce, black vinegar and sesame oil. Let cook for at least 1 hour.

4. Marinate lean pork and pork liver separately with 1 tsp light soy sauce, $1/8$ tsp pepper and $1/4$ tsp cornflour. Marinate minced pork with 1 Tbsp light soy sauce, $1/4$ tsp pepper, $1/2$ tsp cornflour and 1 tsp sesame oil.

5. Strain meat stock back into pot. Add pork meatballs, sugar and salt. Bring to a boil.

6. Prepare each serving of *bak chor mee* separately. Mix pork lard, light soy sauce, black vinegar, fish sauce, chilli paste and braised mushroom sauce for noodle sauce in a serving bowl. Set aside.

7. Blanch a quarter of *mee pok* and a quarter of bean sprouts in a pot of boiling water for 2 minutes. Drain and add to serving bowl. Toss well with sauce.

8. Place a quarter each of marinated mince pork, lean pork and pork liver in a small pot. Add a ladleful of hot meat stock to break up minced pork. Transfer mixture to a strainer and blanch in hot meat stock for 1 minute to cook meat. Drain and add to serving bowl.

9. Add lettuce and a few slices of braised mushrooms to serving bowl.

10. Garnish with fried pork lard and chopped spring onions.

11. Repeat to prepare another 3 servings. Serve hot with meat stock on the side.

Image on page 26

Bak Chor Mee

Hainanese Chicken Rice

Hainanese chicken rice is a favourite to us Singaporean food lovers,
and this recipe is the result of countless tests and try-outs.
When paired with the right chilli sauce, this dish is unforgettable!

HAINANESE CHICKEN RICE

Serves 6

CHICKEN

1 large chicken, about
   1.6 kg (3 lb 9 oz)

2.5-cm (1-in) knob ginger,
   peeled and sliced

1 bunch spring onions
   (scallions)

1–2 Tbsp salt

RICE

600 g (1 lb 5$^1/_3$ oz) uncooked
   jasmine rice

6 Tbsp rendered chicken fat

8 cloves garlic, peeled
   and mashed

2.5-cm (1-in) knob ginger,
   peeled and thickly sliced

800 ml (26$^2/_3$ fl oz) chicken
   stock (from cooking
   chicken)

3–4 pandan leaves, knotted

A large pinch of salt
   or to taste

CHILLI SAUCE

80 g (2$^4/_5$ oz) red chillies

20 g ($^2/_3$ oz) bird's eye chillies

40 g (1$^1/_3$ oz) ginger, peeled

6 cloves garlic, peeled

4 tsp lime juice

4 tsp white vinegar

4 tsp chicken stock
   (from cooking chicken)

1 tsp salt

1 Tbsp sugar

2 Tbsp rendered chicken fat

1 Tbsp sesame oil

DRESSING

4 Tbsp light soy sauce

2 tsp sesame oil

2 Tbsp rendered chicken fat

1 tsp sugar

GARNISH

Sliced cucumber

Chopped coriander leaves
   (cilantro)

Sliced tomatoes

1. Prepare chicken. Fill a large pot with water and add ginger, spring onions and salt. Bring to a boil.

2. When stock is boiling, hold chicken by the neck and ladle hot soup onto it. Continue to scald chicken for about 10 minutes until skin looks cooked.

3. Lower chicken into the boiling water, thigh side down, and cover pot with a lid.

4. Let water return to the boil, then remove lid and lower heat to simmer for 10 minutes.

5. Replace lid, turn off heat and let chicken cook in residual heat for 45 minutes.

6. After 45 minutes, remove chicken and submerge in a basin of iced water for 15 minutes. This step is CRUCIAL as it stops the cooking process and helps the gelatin develop under the chicken skin.

7. Prepare rice. Wash and drain rice. Place into a rice cooker pot. Set aside.

8. Heat chicken fat in a wok over medium heat. Add garlic and ginger and stir-fry until fragrant. Pour mixture over rice in rice cooker.

9. Add chicken stock, pandan leaves and salt to rice and turn on rice cooker to cook rice.

10. When rice is cooked, remove aromatics and give rice a good fluff.

11. Prepare chilli sauce. Place all ingredients except chicken fat and sesame oil in a blender and process until mixture is of a smoothie-like consistency.

12. Transfer chilli sauce to bowl, then mix in chicken fat and sesame oil with a spoon.

13. Mix ingredients for dressing in a bowl.

14. Chop chicken and arrange over a bed of cucumber slices. Pour dressing over and top with coriander leaves and sliced tomatoes.

15. Serve chicken with steamed rice and chilli sauce. Add some minced ginger to chilli sauce and drizzle thick sweet sauce over rice if desired.

Image on page 27

Nasi lemak is an all-time favourite dish that can be enjoyed at almost any time of the day. There are a few things we would expect in a good *nasi lemak* other than the rice, and the most important is the sambal chilli, as we all tend to take lots of it with the *nasi lemak*.

NASI LEMAK COCONUT RICE

Serves 5

RICE
380 g (12²/₃ oz) uncooked rice
250 ml (8 fl oz / 1 cup) coconut milk
450 ml (15 fl oz) water
5 pandan leaves, knotted
2 tsp salt or to taste

SAMBAL CHILLI
20 shallots, peeled
2 onions, peeled
6 cloves garlic, peeled
250 ml (8 fl oz / 1 cup) cooking oil
300 g (11 oz) dried chilli paste
50 g (1³/₄ oz) palm sugar, chopped
80 g (2⁴/₅ oz) sugar or to taste
1 Tbsp salt or to taste

FRIED IKAN KUNING
10 *ikan kuning* (yellowstripe scad)
¹/₂ tsp salt
¹/₂ tsp ground white pepper
1 tsp turmeric powder

FRIED CHICKEN WINGS
5 large chicken wings
1 tsp fennel powder
1 tsp cumin powder
1 tsp coriander powder
1 tsp turmeric powder
¹/₂ tsp ground white pepper
¹/₄ tsp chilli powder
1 tsp salt
1 Tbsp cornflour
1 Tbsp rice flour
100 ml (3¹/₂ fl oz) coconut cream

TOPPING
Fried *ikan bilis* (dried anchovies)
Fried peanuts
Sliced cucumber

1. Marinate *ikan kuning* with salt, pepper and turmeric powder. Mix well, cover and let sit in the fridge for 2 hours.

2. Marinate chicken wings with spices, salt, cornflour, rice flour and coconut cream. Mix well, cover and let sit in the fridge for 2 hours or longer.

3. Prepare rice. Wash and drain rice. Place into a rice cooker pot. Add coconut milk, water, pandan leaves and salt to rice and turn on rice cooker. When rice is cooked, give it a good fluff.

4. Prepare sambal chilli. Blend shallots, onions and garlic in a food processor until fine.

5. Heat oil in a pan over low heat. Add blended shallot mixture to pan and cook over low heat for about 10 minutes or until shallot mixture turns translucent.

6. Add dried chilli paste, palm sugar, sugar and salt. Cook, stirring constantly for 20 minutes. Remove and set aside.

7. When ready to cook *ikan kuning* and chicken wings, heat about 500 ml (16 fl oz 2 cups) oil in a wok to 180°C. Gently lower marinated *ikan kuning* into hot oil and deep-fry for 6–8 minutes until fish is cooked and golden brown. Remove and drain well on paper towels.

8. Repeat to deep-fry marinated chicken wings for 7–10 minutes until chicken is golden brown. Remove one wing and cut the thickest end to check that it is cooked through. Return wing to hot oil to cook longer if necessary. Once done, remove and drain well on paper towels.

9. Once all the elements to the dish are done, serve buffet style or portion out individually.

Satay bee hoon is a fusion of Malay and Chinese food cultures.
The result is a sweet and savoury dish with marvellous flavours and crunch from the
peanut sauce and other key ingredients, including cuttlefish, prawns, *tau pok* and *kang kong*.

SATAY BEE HOON

Serves 4

200 g (7 oz) dried *bee hoon* (rice vermicelli)

1 processed cuttlefish

1 Tbsp salt

5 kaffir lime leaves

200 g *kang kong* (water convolvulus), washed and cut into 5-cm (2-in) lengths

20 medium prawns, peeled and deveined

4 *tau pok* (fried tofu puffs), toasted and cut into strips

2 green chillies, sliced

SATAY GRAVY

500 g (1 lb 1¹/₂ oz) peanuts

4 Tbsp cooking oil

5 Tbsp dried chilli paste

4 Tbsp tamarind paste mixed with 4 Tbsp warm water

1 tsp salt or to taste

2 litres (64 fl oz / 8 cups) boiling water

3 stalks lemongrass, ends trimmed and bruised

5 kaffir lime leaves

100 g (3¹/₂ oz) palm sugar

2 Tbsp fresh chilli paste

125 ml (4 fl oz/ ¹/₂ cup) *kecap manis* (Indonesian sweet soy sauce)

2 Tbsp sugar or to taste

SPICE PASTE

2 large red onions, peeled

12 cloves garlic, peeled

40 g (1¹/₃ oz) galangal, peeled

1 Tbsp fennel seeds

1 Tbsp cumin seeds

6 candlenuts

20 g (²/₃ oz) *belacan* (dried shrimp paste)

1. Prepare satay gravy. Blend peanuts coarsely in a food processor. Remove half to a bowl and blend the remainder until fine. Remove and set aside.

2. Combine all ingredients for spice paste in the food processor and blend into a fine paste.

3. Heat oil in a pot and stir-fry spice paste until fragrant.

4. Add *belacan* and tamarind water and mix well. Season with salt.

5. Add boiling water, lemongrass, kaffir lime leaves, palm sugar and fresh chilli paste. Bring to boil, then add finely ground peanuts and let cook for 10 minutes.

6. Add rest of ground peanuts, *kecap manis* and sugar. Mix well and bring to a boil. Let cook for another 10 minutes, then turn off heat and set aside.

7. Soak dried bee hoon in hot water for 30 minutes. Drain and set aside.

8. In the meantime, wash processed cuttlefish with salt and peel skin from outer layer. Pat dry cuttlefish. Score outer side with criss cross cuts, then cut into 2-cm (³/₄-in) strips.

9. Boil a pot of water and add salt and kaffir lime leaves. Add *kang kong* and soaked *bee hoon* and blanch for 2 minutes. Drain and divide among 4 serving plates.

10. Return water to the boil and blanch cuttlefish and prawns for 2 minutes. Drain and divide among serving plates.

11. Top each plate with *tau pok*, then ladle some satay gravy over. Garnish with sliced green chillies and serve.

Nyonya laksa is also known locally as Katong laksa, where the dish is said to have originated. Like chicken rice and *char kway teow*, it is a local favourite and after eating it for so many years, we decided to find out how it is made. This recipe is the result of many hours of research. Enjoy!

NYONYA LAKSA

Serves 5

200 ml (6³⁄₄ fl oz) peanut oil

750 g (1 lb 11 oz) fresh thick *bee hoon* (rice vermicelli)

500 g (1 lb ¹⁄₁₂ oz) bean sprouts, trimmed

SPICE PASTE

20 dried chillies

100 g (3¹⁄₂ oz) dried shrimp

200 g (7 oz) shallots, peeled

5 red chillies

5 cloves garlic, peeled

30 g (1 oz) turmeric, peeled

50 g (1³⁄₄ oz) galangal, peeled

30 g (1 oz) ginger, peeled

5 stalks lemongrass, white portion only

5 candlenuts

1 Tbsp coriander powder

30 g (1 oz) toasted *belacan* (dried shrimp paste)

LAKSA STOCK

200 ml (6³⁄₄ fl oz) water from soaking dried shrimp

1.5 litres (48 fl oz / 6 cups) packaged fish/prawn stock

5 stalks laksa leaves

1 litre (32 fl oz / 4 cups) coconut milk

2 Tbsp salt or to taste

2 Tbsp sugar

TOPPING

500 g (1 lb ¹⁄₁₂ oz) large prawns, cleaned and trimmed

10 *tau pok* (fried tofu puffs), sliced in half

200 g (7 oz) fish cake, sliced

50 g (1³⁄₄ oz) laksa leaves, finely chopped

1. Prepare spice paste. Remove seeds from dried chillies, then soak chillies in hot water for 30 minutes. Drain before using. Soak dried shrimp in 200 ml (6³⁄₄ fl oz) hot water for 30 minutes, Remove dried prawns. Strain soaking liquid and reserve.

2. Place soaked dried chillies and dried shrimp in a blender with remaining ingredients for spice paste and process until fine.

3. Heat oil in a wok over medium heat. Add spice paste and stir-fry for 30 minutes until colour starts to darken and paste is fragrant.

4. Prepare laksa stock. In a pot, bring reserved liquid from soaking dried shrimp and fish/prawn stock to a boil.

5. Add prawns for topping to stock and cook lightly. Drain and set aside.

6. Add spice paste to stock and mix well. Return stock to a boil and add laksa leaves. Lower heat and simmer for 30 minutes.

7. Add coconut milk and return stock to a boil. When stock is boiling, turn off heat and season with salt and sugar.

8. Add *tau pok* and keep stock warm.

9. Prepare each serving of laksa separately. Blanch a fifth of fresh thick *bee hoon*, a handful of bean sprouts and a few slices of fish cake in a pot of boiling water for 2 minutes. Drain well, making sure to drain as much water as possible. Place in a serving bowl. Ladle laksa stock over with a few slices of *tau pok*. Top with prawns and chopped laksa leaves.

10. Repeat to prepare another 4 servings. Serve hot.

Our version of claypot rice makes use of salted mackerel in oil as they are less salty than dried ones and much softer in terms of texture. Mix this up with quality jasmine rice and dark soy sauce for a claypot feast at home!

CLAYPOT RICE

Serves 6

5 Tbsp cooking oil or oil from salted fish

4–6 slices *mui heong* salted fish (mackerel in oil), cut into cubes

1 *lup cheong* (Chinese wine sausage), sliced

20 g (2/3 oz) chopped ginger

20 g (2/3 oz) chopped garlic

570 g (19 oz) uncooked rice, washed and drained

750 ml (24 fl oz / 3 cups) packaged chicken stock

150 g (5 1/3 oz) choy sum

30 g (1 oz) chopped spring onions

CHICKEN

500 g (1 lb 1 1/2 oz) boneless chicken thigh

2 Tbsp thick dark soy sauce

2 Tbsp oyster sauce

1 Tbsp sesame oil

1 Tbsp cornflour

250 ml (8 fl oz / 1 cup) water

SAUCE

1 Tbsp thick dark soy sauce

1 Tbsp light soy sauce

1/4 tsp ground white pepper

1 Tbsp Chinese rice wine (*hua tiao jiu*)

1 Tbsp oyster sauce

1 tsp sesame oil

1 Tbsp sugar

1. Prepare chicken. Cut boneless chicken thighs into 4-cm chunks and marinate with thick dark soy sauce, oyster sauce, sesame oil, cornflour and water. Mix well, cover and let sit in the fridge for 2 hours or longer.

2. Heat 2 Tbsp oil in a pan over medium heat. Add salted fish and *lup cheong* and stir-fry until fragrant. Set aside.

3. Heat remaining 3 Tbsp oil in a clay pot over medium heat. Add chopped ginger and garlic and stir-fry until fragrant.

4. Add rice and chicken stock to clay pot and bring to a boil. Cover clay pot and let rice cook over medium heat for 10 minutes.

5. After 10 minutes, stir rice. Replace lid and let rice cook for another 10 minutes and stir again.

6. Add salted fish, lup cheong and marinated chicken. Cover and let cook for another 15 minutes.

7. Mix ingredients for sauce in a bowl.

8. Add choy sum to clay pot and pour sauce over ingredients.

9. Cover clay pot and remove from heat. Let sit for 10 minutes.

10. Sprinkle with chopped spring onions before serving.

Braised. Thick. Heavy. These are the key words people associate with *lor mee*,
and it's all true! And it's so damn *shiok*! If you're a fan of braised dishes
with that dark gooey sauce, you'll love this *lor mee* recipe.

LOR MEE

Serves 6

1.2 kg (2 lb 11 oz) flat yellow noodles

180 g (6 oz) bean sprouts, trimmed

Chopped Chinese celery

Sliced red chillies

Chinese black vinegar

GRAVY

1 litre (32 fl oz / 4 cups) water

250 ml (8 fl oz / 1 cup) dark soy sauce

50 g (1³/₄ oz) rock sugar

6 cloves garlic, peeled and sliced

40 g (1¹/₃ oz) ginger, peeled and sliced

2 Tbsp five-spice powder

500 g (1 lb 1¹/₂ oz) pork belly

6 hard-boiled eggs, peeled

125 ml (4 fl oz / ¹/₂ cup) Chinese black vinegar

1 tsp salt or to taste

1 Tbsp sugar or to taste

2 Tbsp light soy sauce

3 eggs

50 g (1³/₄ oz) tapioca starch mixed with 125 ml (4 fl oz / ¹/₂ cup) water

FRIED FISH

400 g (14¹/₃ oz) snakehead fish fillet, cut into 5-cm (2-in) chunks

¹/₄ tsp salt

¹/₄ tsp ground white pepper

¹/₂ tsp sesame oil

2 Tbsp plain flour

1 egg white

500 ml (16 fl oz / 2 cups) cooking oil

1. Prepare gravy. Place water, dark soy sauce, rock sugar, garlic, ginger and five-spice powder in a large pot. Bring to a boil and add pork belly. Lower heat and simmer for 20 minutes.

2. Add hard-boiled eggs and simmer for another 20 minutes.

3. Remove braised pork belly and hard-boiled eggs and set aside.

4. Strain gravy back into pot. Discard ginger and garlic.

5. Add Chinese black vinegar, salt, sugar and light soy sauce to gravy and stir to mix.

6. Crack eggs into a bowl and beat lightly. Add to gravy in a slow and steady stream while stirring gravy.

7. Place pot over low heat and add tapioca starch solution to thicken gravy.

8. In the meantime, prepare fried fish. Mix fish fillet with salt, pepper, sesame oil, plain flour and egg white. Ensure fish is evenly coated.

9. Heat oil over medium heat. Add fish and deep-fry for 4–6 minutes or until fish is golden brown. Remove and drain well on paper towels.

10. Cut braised pork belly into 2-cm (³/₄-in) strips and hard-boiled eggs into halves.

11. Prepare each serving of *lor mee* separately. Blanch a sixth of yellow noodles and bean sprouts in boiling water for 2–3 minutes. Drain and place in a serving bowl. Ladle gravy over to cover noodles, then top with 2 hard-boiled egg halves, strips of braised pork belly and a few pieces of fried fish. Garnish with chopped Chinese celery and sliced red chillies.

12. Repeat to prepare another 5 servings.

13. Offer more Chinese black vinegar on the side for diners to add as desired.

It comes as no secret that a good bowl of prawn noodles lies in a few factors —
the texture of the noodles, prawns cooked just right, fork- (or rather chopstick-) tender pork ribs
and last but not least, a flavourful BROTH.

PRAWN NOODLE SOUP

Serves 4

1 kg (2 lb 3 oz) large prawns

500 g (1 lb 1¹/₂ oz) pork ribs

800 g (1³/₄ lb) round yellow
   noodles

100 g (3¹/₂ oz) bean sprouts,
   trimmed

200 g (7 oz) *kang kong*
   (water convolvulus),
   washed and cut into
   5-cm (2-in) lengths

50 g (1³/₄ oz) fried shallots

Chilli powder

Chopped coriander leaves
   (cilantro)

SOUP STOCK

4 Tbsp cooking oil

4 cloves garlic, peeled
   and sliced

Prawn heads and shells

2 litres (64 fl oz / 8 cups)
   boiling water

2 star anise

5 cloves

80 g (2⁴/₅ oz) *ikan bilis*
   (dried anchovies)

3 Tbsp brown sugar

30 g (1 oz) rock sugar

2 Tbsp white peppercorns

1 Tbsp fish sauce

¹/₄ tsp ground white pepper

1 Tbsp dark soy sauce

1 Tbsp salt or to taste

1. Wash and devein prawns. Peel and set heads and shells aside for use in stock.

2. Blanch pork ribs in hot water. Drain and set aside.

3. Prepare soup stock. Heat oil in a pot over medium heat. Add garlic and stir-fry until fragrant. Add prawn heads and shells and stir-fry until they turn red.

4. Add pork ribs and all remaining ingredients for soup stock. Bring to a boil, then lower heat and simmer for at least 2 hours.

5. Strain stock back into pot. Pick out pork ribs and set aside. Discard other ingredients. Skim fat from stock.

6. Return stock to the boil and blanch prawns for 2–3 minutes being careful not to overcook prawns so they stay crisp and firm.

7. Taste and adjust seasoning of stock with salt if necessary.

8. Prepare each serving of noodles separately. Blanch a quarter of yellow noodles, bean sprouts and *kang kong* in a pot of boiling water. Drain and place in a serving bowl. Add a few pork ribs and prawns to bowl and top with soup stock.

9. Repeat to prepare another 3 servings.

10. Garnish with a dash of chilli powder and some chopped coriander leaves. Serve with cut red chillies in light soy sauce on the side if desired.

Hainanese pork chop is delicious! To start off, pound the pork chop with a mallet or the back of your cleaver to tenderise it. Then marinate it for at least an hour, or if you have the time, the longer the better! This process adds flavour to the meat.

HAINANESE PORK CHOP RICE

Serves 6

600 g (1 lb 5$^1/_3$ oz) pork loin

18 cream crackers

2 eggs, beaten

Cooking oil for deep-frying

Cooked rice

MARINADE

$^1/_2$ tsp baking soda (optional if marinating overnight)

1 tsp five-spice powder

1 Tbsp sugar

1 Tbsp minced garlic

2 Tbsp *tau cheo* (fermented soy bean paste)

1 tsp sesame oil

1 Tbsp light soy sauce

1 Tbsp cornflour, mixed with 2 Tbsp water

SAUCE

2 Tbsp cooking oil

1 Tbsp minced garlic

1 red onion, peeled and sliced

50 g (1$^3/_4$ oz) frozen mixed vegetables (corn, peas and carrots)

1 Tbsp light soy sauce

1 Tbsp Worcestershire sauce

1 Tbsp A1 steak sauce

3 Tbsp tomato ketchup

$^1/_4$ tsp ground white pepper

1 Tbsp sugar

1 Tbsp Chinese rice wine (*hua tiao jiu*) (optional)

250 ml (8 fl oz / 1 cup) water

1 Tbsp cornflour, mixed with 2 Tbsp water

1. Cut pork loin equally into 6 slices. Butterfly each slice and flatten with a meat tenderiser.

2. Mix ingredients for marinade in a bowl and rub over pork loin. Mix well, cover and let sit for 1 hour.

3. Blend cream crackers in a food processor until fine. Transfer to a flat tray and spread crumbs out.

4. Mix ingredients for sauce in a bowl. Set aside.

5. Add beaten eggs to marinated pork loin and mix well.

6. Place pork loin into tray of cracker crumbs and coat well.

7. Heat sufficient oil for deep-frying in a wok over medium heat. Gently lower pork loin into hot oil and deep-fry pork until golden brown. Remove and set aside to drain.

8. In the meantime, prepare sauce. Heat oil in a pan over medium heat. Add minced garlic, onion and mixed vegetables. Stir-fry until onion is translucent.

9. Add remaining ingredients for sauce and bring to a boil. When sauce starts to thicken, turn off heat.

10. To serve, spoon rice onto serving plates. Slice pork chop and arrange on serving plates. Ladle sauce over pork chop.

Fishball noodle soup is a healthy, light-tasting and
easy one-dish meal. Not only is this dish tasty and super yummy,
it is also a healthy alternative to many Asian dishes!

FISHBALL NOODLE SOUP

Serves 2

1 litre (32 fl oz / 4 cups) fish or *ikan bilis* (dried anchovies) stock

10 fishballs

1 large fried fish cake, thinly sliced

300 g (11 oz) yellow noodles or *mee pok* (flat egg noodles)

60 g (2 oz) bean sprouts, trimmed

2 lettuce leaves

2 Tbsp fried shallots

2 Tbsp chopped spring onions (scallions)

MINCED MEAT TOPPING

100 g ($3^{1}/_{2}$ oz) minced pork

1 Tbsp sesame oil

1 tsp light soy sauce

$^{1}/_{2}$ tsp ground white pepper

3 Tbsp water

NOODLE SAUCE (PER SERVING)

1 tsp black vinegar

$^{1}/_{2}$ tsp fish sauce

$^{1}/_{2}$ tsp light soy sauce

1 Tbsp fried pork lard with oil

1 Tbsp ketchup or sambal chilli

1 Tbsp fish or *ikan bilis* (dried anchovy) stock

1. Prepare minced meat topping. Place minced pork, sesame oil, light soy sauce, pepper and water in a small pot. Mix well and cook over low heat for about 15 minutes. Set aside.

2. Bring fish or *ikan bilis* stock to a boil. Add fishballs and cook for 5 minutes. Turn heat to low.

3. Prepare noodle sauce. Add black vinegar, fish sauce, light soy sauce, fried pork lard with oil, ketchup or sambal chilli and stock to a serving bowl. Mix well and set aside.

4. Blanch half the yellow noodles and half the bean sprouts in a pot of boiling water for 1–2 minutes. Drain and add to serving bowl. Toss to coat with sauce.

5. Top noodles with 5 fishballs, a few slices of fish cake and 2 Tbsp minced meat topping.

6. Add lettuce and garnish with fried shallots and chopped spring onions.

7. Repeat to prepare another serving.

8. Serve hot with stock and cut red chillies in light soy sauce on the side if desired.

MEAT AND SEAFOOD

Bak kut teh (BKT) was brought into Singapore by the Chinese immigrants and there are two versions of it, a peppery one and a herbal one. Our variant of BKT is the former, or the iconic Singapore version that combines sweet pork ribs with aromatic garlic and white peppercorns.

BAK KUT TEH PORK RIB SOUP

Serves 4

1 kg (2 lb 3 oz) pork ribs

2 kg (4 lb 6 oz) pork bones

4 bulbs garlic

100 g (3^1/$_2$ oz) white peppercorns

2.5 litres (80 fl oz / 10 cups) boiling water

1 Tbsp salt

Chopped coriander leaves (cilantro)

4 *you tiao* (fried Chinese crullers)

Sliced red chillies

Dark soy sauce

1. Boil a pot of water and blanch pork ribs and bones briefly. Drain and set aside.

2. Heat a pan over medium heat and dry-roast garlic and peppercorns separately.

3. Wrap peppercorns in cheese cloth and place in a large pot. Add garlic and boiling water.

4. Add pork ribs and bones and salt. Bring to a boil, then lower heat and simmer for 2–2^1/$_2$ hours or until meat is starting to fall off the bone.

5. Dish out and garnish with coriander. Serve hot with rice and *you tiao*. Offer sliced red chillies and dark soy sauce on the side.

People who love *rojak* (page 70) will very likely also be big on cuttlefish *kang kong*.
It's refreshing to have the blanched cuttlefish mixed together with *kang kong*,
and topped with the spicy yet sweet peanut sauce.

CUTTLEFISH KANG KONG

Serves 4

1 processed cuttlefish

1 Tbsp salt

2 Tbsp *hoi sin* sauce

2 Tbsp *haeko*
(black prawn paste)

2 Tbsp plum sauce

1 tsp *sambal belacan*

1/2 tsp sugar

2 Tbsp water

Juice from 1 calamansi lime

200 g (7 oz) *kang kong* (water
convolvulus), washed and
cut into 5-cm (2-in) lengths

2 Tbsp white sesame seeds,
toasted

2 Tbsp ground peanuts

1. Wash processed cuttlefish with salt and peel skin
from outer layer. Pat dry cuttlefish. Score outer side
with criss cross cuts, then cut into 2-cm (3/4-in) strips.

2. In a bowl, mix together *hoi sin* sauce, *haeko*, plum
sauce, *sambal belacan*, sugar, water and lime juice.
Set aside.

3. Boil a pot of water and blanch *kang kong* for about
2 minutes or until *kang kong* darkens. Drain and
arrange on a serving plate.

4. Return water to the boil and blanch cuttlefish for
2 minutes. Drain and add to serving plate.

5. Pour sauce mixture over cuttlefish and *kang kong*.
Top with toasted white sesame seeds and ground
peanuts. Serve.

When creating this dish at home, patience is key, as most household stoves won't get hot enough to achieve the crisping as quickly as the industrial quality stoves used by hawkers. Get yourself 10 large, fresh oysters to add freshness to the crispy batter for the ultimate ooomph!

ORH LUAK OYSTER OMELETTE

Serves 1

3 Tbsp tapioca flour

1 Tbsp rice flour

A pinch of salt

100 ml (3¹/₂ fl oz) water

1 Tbsp Chinese rice wine (*hua tiao jiu*)

1 Tbsp fish sauce

1 tsp light soy sauce

2 eggs

4 Tbsp pork lard

10 large oysters (fresh or frozen)

2 Tbsp chopped spring onion (scallion)

Coriander leaves (cilantro)

1. In a bowl, mix together tapioca flour, rice flour, salt and water.

2. In another bowl, mix together rice wine, fish sauce and light soy sauce.

3. In a third bowl, beat eggs and season with 1 Tbsp sauce mixture. Mix well.

4. Heat 3 Tbsp pork lard in a hot pan.

5. Add batter a small ladleful at a time to pan. Let batter cook until it is crisp on both sides.

6. Add half the egg mixture to pan and let egg cook.

7. Flip cooked batter over and add remaining egg mixture. Let egg cook.

8. Break cooked batter into small pieces and push to one side of pan.

9. Add remaining 1 Tbsp pork lard to other side of pan.

10. Add oysters and season with remaining sauce mixture. Let cook for 30 seconds, then toss with cooked batter.

11. Add chopped spring onion and coriander leaves. Dish out and serve hot.

Satay is a dish of grilled skewered meat that is eaten with a fragrant peanut sauce.
Another hawker hero, satay is available at most hawker centres all over sunny Singapore
and there are now companies that specialise in supplying frozen satay.

SATAY

Serves 4

SATAY

600 g (1 lb 5$^1/_3$ oz) chicken thigh
  meat, pork, beef or mutton
Bamboo skewers, as needed

MARINADE

2 stalks lemongrass
12 shallots, peeled
2 Tbsp minced garlic
2 Tbsp ginger juice
2 Tbsp coriander powder
1 Tbsp cumin powder
1 Tbsp turmeric powder
1 tsp salt
6 Tbsp sugar
2 Tbsp sweet dark soy sauce
4 Tbsp peanut oil

PEANUT SAUCE PART A

250 g (9 oz) toasted ground
  peanuts
40 g (1$^1/_3$ oz) tamarind paste
  mixed with 250 ml (8 fl oz /
  1 cup) hot water
100 ml (3$^1/_2$ fl oz) water

PEANUT SAUCE PART B

1 stalk lemongrass
6 shallots, peeled
3 cloves garlic, peeled
3 slices ginger
6 dried red chillies
3 Tbsp peanut oil
4 Tbsp sugar
1 Tbsp sweet dark soy sauce

OPTIONAL SIDES

Pineapple purée
Ketupat (rice cakes)
Sliced cucumbers and onions

1. Start preparations a day ahead.

2. Cut meat into strips about 2.5-cm (1-in) wide.

3. Remove tough outer leaves from lemongrass and trim ends. Cut into short lengths and place in a food processor with rest of ingredients for marinade. Blend into a smooth paste.

4. Add marinade paste to meat and mix well. Cover and let sit in the fridge overnight.

5. Soak bamboo skewers in water for 20 minutes to prevent them from burning when grilled. Thread marinated meat onto bamboo skewers. Set aside.

6. Prepare peanut sauce. Place ingredients for peanut sauce part B in a food processor and blend into a smooth paste. Transfer to a pot and add ingredients for peanut sauce part A. Bring mixture to a boil, then lower heat and simmer for 20 minutes.

7. Grill satay on a charcoal grill for 4–5 minutes on each side or until meat is cooked through.

8. Serve satay with satay sauce on the side. Top sauce with pineapple purée and offer optional sides such as *ketupat*, sliced cucumber and/or sliced onions if desired.

This is none other than the famous Singapore chilli crab!
It is undoubtedly the flavourful combination of the sweet and spicy sauce
that makes chilli crab one of Singapore's national favourites.

CHILLI CRAB

Serves 4

2 mud crabs

Coriander leaves (cilantro)

16 fried *mantou* (steamed buns)

SAUCE

5 Tbsp cooking oil

1 tsp *tau cheo* (fermented soy bean paste)

3 Tbsp sugar

$1/2$ tsp salt

5 Tbsp tomato ketchup

250 ml (8 fl oz / 1 cup) boiling water

2 eggs, beaten

CHILLI PASTE

5 shallots, peeled

5 cloves garlic, peeled

5 red chillies, seeds removed

8 dried chillies, seeds removed and rehydrated in water

1 stalk lemongrass

6 candlenuts

4 slices galangal

1 green lime

2 Tbsp *belacan* (dried prawn paste), toasted

1. Clean crabs and remove gills. Cut into quarters. Set aside.

2. Prepare sauce. Place all ingredients for chilli paste in a food processor and blend into a smooth paste.

3. Heat oil in a wok over medium heat. Add chilli paste and stir-fry until aromatic.

4. Add *tau cheo*, sugar, salt and tomato ketchup. Mix well.

5. Add crabs and mix to coat crabs with sauce.

6. Add boiling water and cover wok with a lid. Lower heat and simmer for 8–12 minutes, until crabs turn bright red.

7. Slowly stir beaten eggs into sauce. Let cook for 1–2 minutes.

8. Dish out and garnish with coriander leaves. Serve with fried *mantou*.

Love eating crabs but don't wanna to spend a bomb on it? Now you can, with our recipe for black pepper crab! This is one of those things that can be bad for you if you have too much of it, BUT like all good things in life, the price you pay is well worth it! Enjoy!

BLACK PEPPER CRAB

Serves 4

2 Sri Lankan mud crabs, each about 800 g (1³/₄ lb)

3 Tbsp black peppercorns

1 Tbsp white peppercorns

Cooking oil for deep-frying

60 g (2 oz) butter

3 Tbsp chopped garlic

3 Tbsp chopped shallots

¹/₂ cup curry leaves

2 Tbsp sliced bird's eye chillies (*cili padi*)

3 Tbsp oyster sauce

3 Tbsp light soy sauce

3 Tbsp sugar

100 ml (3¹/₂ fl oz) water

Coriander leaves (cilantro)

1. Clean crabs and remove gills. Cut into quarters. Set aside.

2. Heat a pan over medium heat and dry-roast black and white peppercorns until fragrant. Using a spice mill, grind peppercorns coarsely.

3. Heat oil for deep-frying in a wok over medium heat. Add crabs and deep-fry for 3 minutes or until they turn bright red. Remove and drain well.

4. Drain oil from wok and add butter. Add garlic, shallots, ground peppercorns, curry leaves and chillies. Stir-fry until fragrant.

5. Add oyster sauce, light soy sauce, sugar and water.

6. Add crabs and stir-fry for 5–7 minutes.

7. Dish out and garnish with coriander leaves. Serve hot.

Sambal stingray must be one of the most popular dishes that locals would order from a seafood *zi char* stall! Singaporeans LOVE spicy flavours, and the way the sambal chilli blends so perfectly with the stingray makes it completely irresistible!

SAMBAL STINGRAY

Serves 2

Cooking oil as needed

1 stingray wing, about 500 g (1 lb 1½ oz)

1 tsp salt

2 sheets banana leaf, each about 30-cm square

5 shallots, peeled and sliced

Coriander leaves (cilantro)

4 calamansi limes

SAMBAL CHILLI

20 g (²/₃ oz) dried chillies, seeds removed and rehydrated in water

20 g (²/₃ oz) *belacan* (dried prawn paste), toasted

80 g (2⁴/₅ oz) red chillies

150 g (5¹/₃ oz) shallots, peeled

60 g (2 oz) garlic, peeled

40 g (1¹/₃ oz) lemongrass, sliced

25 g (⁴/₅ oz) ginger, peeled and sliced

40 g (1¹/₃ oz) palm sugar

2 Tbsp tamarind pulp mixed with 3 Tbsp hot water

1 tsp salt

1. Prepare sambal chilli. Place all ingredients for sambal chilli into a food processor and blend into a smooth paste.

2. Heat 100 ml (3½ fl oz) oil in a pan over medium heat. Add sambal chilli and stir-fry until oil starts to separate from paste. Set aside to cool.

3. Rinse and pat dry stingray wing. Cut slits on both sides and season with salt.

4. Heat 3 tsp oil in a pan over medium heat. Place a sheet of banana leaf on pan.

5. Spread sambal chilli over one side of stingray wing and place sambal-side down on banana leaf in pan. Cover pan and cook for 5–6 minutes.

6. Spread sambal chilli on uncoated side of stingray wing and sprinkle with sliced onions. Cover with remaining sheet of banana leaf and flip stingray over so new banana leaf is now in direct contact with pan. Cover and cook for 5–6 minutes.

7. Dish out and arrange on a serving plate. Garnish with coriander and serve with calamansi limes.

What makes fish head curry special is how the flavour of the spices infuse the flesh of the fish. Our choice of fish is the red snapper, so get yourself a fresh and fleshy fish head from your friendly neighbourhood fishmonger!

FISH HEAD CURRY, CHINESE-STYLE

Serves 4

4 Tbsp cooking oil

1 Tbsp fenugreek seeds

30 curry leaves

3 Tbsp fish curry powder

800 ml (27 fl oz) water

2 Tbsp tamarind paste mixed with 2 Tbsp warm water

200 ml (7 fl oz) coconut cream

2 Tbsp sugar or to taste

1 Tbsp salt or to taste

1 large red snapper fish head, sliced in half

1 medium aubergine (eggplant), cut into 8-cm (3-in) sticks

6 ladies' fingers, stem end trimmed

100 g (3½ oz) fried tofu skin, cut into 8-cm (3-in) lengths

3 tomatoes, cut into quarters

Coriander leaves (cilantro)

SPICE PASTE

150 g (5⅓ oz) shallots, peeled

15 cloves garlic, peeled

40 g (1⅓ oz) ginger, peeled

40 g (1⅓ oz) galangal, peeled

2 stalks lemongrass, tough outer leaves removed, ends trimmed and sliced

100 g (3½ oz) dried chilli paste

2 Tbsp turmeric powder

100 ml (3½ fl oz) water

1. Prepare spice paste. Place shallots, garlic, ginger, galangal, lemongrass, dried chilli paste, turmeric powder and 100 ml (3½ fl oz) water in a food processor and blend until smooth.

2. Heat oil in a pot over medium heat. Add spice paste and stir-fry for 10 minutes until fragrant.

3. Add fenugreek seeds, curry leaves and fish curry powder and stir-fry for 5 minutes.

4. Add 800 ml (27 fl oz) water, tamarind water and coconut cream. Stir mixture evenly.

5. Season with sugar and salt. Set curry aside.

6. Place fish head in a steamer and steam for about 8 minutes or until fish head is almost done.

7. Bring curry to a boil. Add aubergine, ladies' fingers and fried tofu skin.

8. When aubergine and ladies' fingers start to soften, add tomatoes. Cook for another 2 minutes.

9. Add steamed fish head to curry and cook for another 3 minutes.

10. Garnish with coriander leaves and serve hot.

We Singaporeans love our BBQ chicken wings!
The taste of well-marinated chicken grilled over charcoal just can't be beat!
It's simple to do, and always a hit with anyone young and old!

BBQ CHICKEN WINGS

Makes 12 wings

12 large chicken wings

4 calamansi limes

MARINADE

3 Tbsp oyster sauce

2 Tbsp honey

1 Tbsp sesame oil

1 Tbsp minced garlic

1 tsp coriander powder

1 tsp ground white pepper

1 tsp salt

1 Tbsp light soy sauce

2 Tbsp ginger juice

CHILLI SAUCE

10 red chillies

Juice from 6 calamansi limes

20 g ($^2/_3$ oz) ginger, peeled
  and sliced

50 ml ($1^2/_3$ fl oz) white vinegar

4 Tbsp sugar or to taste

1 Tbsp salt or to taste

1. Combine all ingredients for marinade in a large bowl.

2. Add chicken wings to marinade and mix well. Cover and let sit in the fridge for 4–6 hours.

3. Blend all ingredients for chilli sauce in a food processor. Transfer to a bowl and set aside.

4. Grill chicken wings over a charcoal grill for about 10 minutes, turning them frequently.

5. Once wings start to brown, cover them with aluminium foil and let cook over indirect low heat for another 10 minutes.

6. Arrange chicken wings on a plate. Serve with chilli sauce and calamansi limes.

SNACKS AND DESSERTS

What's great about *popiah* is that it provides a mix of different textures and flavours in a single bite — from the crunch from the peanuts and the fried pork skin, to the fresh and juicy vegetables — and it all goes really well with the sweet flour sauce and spicy sambal.

POPIAH SPRING ROLL

Makes 12

500 g (1 lb 1¹/₂ oz) *popiah* skin

FILLING

1 Tbsp cooking oil

3 cloves garlic, peeled
and chopped

5 shallots, peeled and
chopped

2 large *bangkwang* (yam bean),
peeled and shredded

1 carrot, peeled and shredded

1 Tbsp light soy sauce

1 Tbsp oyster sauce

A dash of ground white pepper

1 Tbsp sugar

250 ml (8 fl oz / 1 cup) water

TOPPINGS

125 ml (4 fl oz / ¹/₂ cup)
sweet flour sauce

1 garlic bulb, peeled
and minced

4 Tbsp sambal chilli

1 small head lettuce

40 g (1¹/₃ oz) bean sprouts,
trimmed and blanched

3 hard-boiled eggs, peeled
and chopped

120 g (4²/₃ oz) ground peanuts

30 g (1 oz) fried pork skin,
crushed

300 g (11 oz) poached prawns,
peeled and sliced

1. Prepare filling. Heat oil in a pot over medium heat. Add garlic and shallots and stir-fry until fragrant.

2. Add *bangkwang* and carrot and stir-fry to mix.

3. Add light soy sauce, oyster sauce, pepper, sugar and water and let it simmer for 20 minutes.

4. Lay 2 sheets of *popiah* skin on a clean and dry work surface.

5. Spoon some sweet flour sauce, garlic and sambal chilli on the centre of *popiah* skin and spread mixture using the back of a spoon.

6. Place a small lettuce leaf over the mixture, then top with a handful of blanched bean sprouts.

7. Drain 2 Tbsp cooked filling and place over bean sprouts.

8. Top with some chopped hard-boiled eggs, ground peanuts, fried pork skin and poached prawns.

9. Fold two opposite sides of popiah skin over filling, then roll up to enclose filling. Slice into 2.5-cm (1-in) thick slices. Repeat to make more rolls. Serve immediately.

Chinese *rojak* is a wonderful mix of sweet and sour flavours
and the crisp and juicy textures of the fruits and vegetables.
The prawn paste, when mixed with the dish, makes it oh so yummy!

CHINESE ROJAK

Serves 4

1 cucumber

1 *bangkwang* (yam bean),
peeled

1 green apple, peeled
and cored

1 small pineapple, peeled

40 g (1 1/3 oz) bean sprouts,
trimmed and blanched

2 *you tiao* (fried Chinese
crullers), toasted

1 *tau pok (*fried tofu puff),
toasted

2 Tbsp toasted ground
peanuts

ROJAK SAUCE

3 Tbsp *haeko* (black prawn
paste)

2 Tbsp tamarind paste,
mixed with 3 Tbsp hot
water

4 Tbsp sugar

1 Tbsp minced red chillies
(optional)

1/2 calamansi lime zest,
finely sliced

Shavings of torch ginger bud

1. In a large mixing bowl, combine all ingredients for
rojak sauce and mix well.

2. Add 10 bite-size wedges of each of these ingredient
to bowl: cucumber, bangkwang, apple and pineapple.

3. Add a handful of bean sprouts.

4. Cut *you tiao* into thick slices and add to bowl.

5. Cut *tau pok* into bite-size pieces and add to bowl.

6. Add ground peanuts and mix until *rojak* sauce coats
all the ingredients.

7. Transfer to a serving plate and with more ground
peanuts. Serve.

Spicy minced fish wrapped in banana leaves and flame-grilled to perfection
— *otak-otak* is a hawker classic that many of us will remember from our childhood days.
Enjoy on its own or as a sandwich filling.

OTAK-OTAK

Makes 12

12 sheets banana leaves,
each 26 x 18-cm (10 x 7-in)

Cooking oil, as needed

24 bamboo toothpicks

OTAK-OTAK PASTE

30 g (1 oz) dried chillies,
seeds removed and soaked
in hot water for 30 minutes

250 g (9 oz) shallots, peeled

25 g ($^4/_5$ oz) galangal, peeled

30 g (1 oz) lemongrass, white
bulbous end only, sliced

10 candlenuts

20 g ($^2/_3$ oz) *belacan*
(dried prawn paste)

1 Tbsp turmeric powder

85 ml (2$^1/_2$ fl oz / $^1/_3$ cup)
cooking oil

1 Tbsp coriander powder

1 Tbsp sugar

1 tsp salt

400 g (14$^1/_3$ oz) *batang*
(Spanish mackerel) fillet

200 g (7 oz) peeled prawns

2 eggs

100 ml (3$^1/_2$ fl oz) coconut
milk

4 kaffir lime leaves, sliced

1. Prepare *otak-otak* paste. Remove seeds from dried chillies, then soak chillies in hot water for 30 minutes. Drain chillies and add to food processor with shallots, galangal, lemongrass, candlenuts, *belacan* and turmeric powder. Blend into a fine paste.

2. Heat oil in a pan over medium heat. Add spice paste, coriander powder, sugar and salt. Stir-fry until oil starts to separate from paste. Transfer paste to a bowl and set aside to cool to room temperature.

3. Add fish and peeled prawns to food processor. Blend into a paste.

4. Add eggs, coconut milk, cooled spice paste and kaffir lime leaves, and blend again.

5. Brush a little oil on the dull side of a sheet of banana leaf. Top with 2 Tbsp *otak-otak* paste and fold 2 long sides of banana leaf over to enclose paste. Secure open ends of parcel with toothpicks. Repeat until ingredients are used up.

6. Grill *otak-otak* parcels for 5–6 minutes on each side or until cooked through.

This fluffy peanut pancake invokes many childhood memories for us.
Who doesn't love a moist and fluffy pancake, stuffed with
a generous portion of crushed peanuts and sugar?

MIN CHIANG KUEH

Serves 4

130 g (4$^1/_3$ oz) plain flour

$^1/_2$ tsp baking soda

$^1/_2$ tsp instant yeast

2 Tbsp sugar

1 egg

160 ml (5$^1/_3$ fl oz) lukewarm
water

FILLING

50 g (1$^3/_4$ oz) roasted ground
peanuts

15 g ($^1/_2$ oz) white sesame
seeds, toasted

25 g ($^4/_5$ oz) sugar

1. Combine flour, baking soda, instant yeast, sugar and egg in a bowl. Add lukewarm water and mix well into a smooth batter. Cover bowl loosely with plastic wrap and set aside to proof for 30 minutes.

2. Prepare filling. Mix ground peanuts, sesame seeds and sugar in a bowl. Set aside.

3. Preheat a non-stick pan over low heat for 10 minutes. Coat pan with a thin layer of oil using a cooking spray or a paper towel dipped in oil.

4. Add sufficient batter to cover base of pan, then cover pan with a lid and let cook for 4 minutes.

5. Remove lid and top pancake with some peanut mixture. Replace lid and let cook for another 2–3 minutes.

6. Fold pan in half and remove from pan. Slice and serve.

Tau suan is a dessert soup made with split mung beans.
These lentils are said to help reduce body heatiness, and we believe that the starchy
and gooey concoction will help warm the stomach as well!

TAU SUAN

Serves 10

500 g (1 lb 1¹/₂ oz) mung beans

10 pandan leaves

80 g (2⁴/₅ oz) sweet potato starch

2 litres (64 fl oz / 8 cups) water

150 g (5¹/₃ oz) sugar or to taste

2 *you tiao* (fried Chinese crullers), toasted and sliced

1. Rinse and soak mung beans in water for 2 hours.

2. Cut 5 pandan leaves into short strips and place some on a steaming tray. Drain mung beans and transfer to steaming tray. Place remaining cut pandan leaves on mung beans and steam for 10 minutes.

3. Mix sweet potato starch with water. Set aside.

4. Bring 2 litres (64 fl oz / 8 cups) water to a boil in a pot. Tie remaining 5 pandan leaves into a knot and add to boiling water.

5. Add sugar and stir.

6. Remove and discard pandan leaf strips from steamed mung beans. Spoon mung beans into pot of boiling water.

7. Let cook for 5 minutes, then slowly add sweet potato starch mixture while stirring until mixture thickens.

8. Ladle *tau suan* into serving bowls and top with *you tiao*. Serve hot.

Cheng tng literally means clear soup in Teochew and this is what sets this cooling and refreshing local dessert apart from the other rich and creamy desserts like *burbur chacha* or *ice kacang* (page 80).

CHENG TNG

Serves 10

8 *pang da hai* (sterculia seeds)

50 g (1³/₄ oz) dried lotus seeds

50 g (1³/₄ oz) dried white fungus

Water, as needed

50 g (1³/₄ oz) pearl barley, rinsed

50 g (1³/₄ oz) large sago

200 g (7 oz) dried longan

100 g (3¹/₂ oz) prepared gingko nuts

50 g (1³/₄ oz) candied winter melon

50 g (1³/₄ oz) brown sugar

50 g (1³/₄ oz) rock sugar

3 pandan leaves, each tied into a knot

1. Soak *pang da hai* in hot water for 30 minutes until seeds expand. Remove and discard skin and pit. Rinse jelly in running water. Drain and set aside.

2. Soak dried lotus seeds in water for 30 minutes. Remove and discard green core.

3. Soak dried white fungus in hot water for 10 minutes until softened, then cut into smaller pieces. Set aside.

4. Bring 2 litres (64 fl oz / 8 cups) water to a boil in a pot. Add pearl barley and large sago and boil until sago is translucent. Drain and set aside.

5. Add 3 litres (96 fl oz / 12 cups) water to another pot. Add pandan leaves and bring to a boil.

6. Add soaked white fungus, dried longan, gingko nuts, soaked lotus seeds, candied winter melon, brown sugar and rock sugar. Boil for 20 minutes for ingredients to soften.

7. Remove pandan leaves and lower heat to a simmer. Add *pang da hai* and let is simmer for another 20 minutes.

8. Serve hot or chilled.

A mountain of shaved ice, drenched in different coloured syrups and sometimes *gula melaka*. Many of us like to dig beneath the 'mountain' for various 'treasures', including sweet red beans, agar-agar cubes and the prized atap seeds. To give this childhood favourite more texture, we've topped it with crushed peanuts.

PEANUT ICE KACANG

Serves 5

150 g (5^1/$_3$ oz) red beans
100 g (3^1/$_2$ oz) sugar
435 ml (14 fl oz / 1^3/$_4$ cups)
   water
Ice cubes

SYRUP

100 g (3^1/$_2$ oz) sugar
Water, as needed
A little red food colouring
A little green food colouring
50 g (1^3/$_4$ oz) brown sugar

TOPPINGS

250 g (9 oz) *cendol* jelly
250 g (9 oz) glass jelly,
   cut into cubes
15 atap seeds (palm seeds)
1 can creamed corn, 400 g
   (14^1/$_3$ oz)
50 g (1^3/$_4$ oz) peanut powder
50 ml (1^3/$_4$ fl oz) evaporated milk

1. Add red beans, sugar and water to a pot. Boil over medium heat for about 2 hours until beans are soft. Drain and set aside.

2. Prepare syrup. Add sugar and 100 ml (3^1/$_2$ fl oz) water to a pot. Boil over medium heat until syrup thickens.

3. Pour syrup into 2 bowls. Add red food colouring to one bowl and green food colouring to the other. Set aside to cool.

4. Repeat to make brown sugar syrup. Add brown sugar and 50 ml (1^3/$_4$ fl oz) water to the pot. Boil over medium heat until syrup thickens. Set aside to cool.

5. Prepare each serving of *ice kacang* separately. Spoon 3 Tbsp cooked red beans, 2 Tbsp *cendol*, 3 Tbsp glass jelly and 3 atap seeds into a serving bowl. Shave ice over ingredients until it forms a cone. Ladle red, green and brown sugar syrup over ice. Top with 2 Tbsp creamed corn and 2 Tbsp peanut powder. Drizzle with evaporated milk and serve.

Roti John is best described as a crispy baguette with an alluring fragrance
from caramelised meat and onions wrapped into a beautiful parcel with golden fried eggs,
drizzled with a ketchup mixture added as a finishing touch.

ROTI JOHN

Serves 2

1/2 large baguette

3 eggs

1 Tbsp sambal chilli

A pinch of ground black
   pepper

1/4 tsp salt

100 g (3 1/2 oz) minced lamb,
   beef or chicken

1/2 tsp cumin powder

2 Tbsp cooking oil

1 Tbsp minced garlic

1/2 onion, peeled and sliced

Cucumber slices

SAUCE

2 Tbsp ketchup

2 Tbsp chilli sauce

2 Tbsp water

1 Tbsp sugar

1. Slice baguette in half, spread it open and toast lightly. Set aside.

2. Beat eggs in a bowl and season with sambal chilli, pepper and salt. Mix well. Set aside.

3. Season meat with cumin powder and mix well. Set aside.

4. Combine ingredients for sauce in a bowl.

5. Heat oil in a pan over low heat. Add garlic and onion, and stir-fry lightly.

6. Add meat and stir-fry until onion is translucent.

7. Spread meat mixture out evenly over base of pan, then pour egg mixture over.

8. Place baguette cut-side down in pan and press down so bread soaks up some of the egg. Let cook for 2 minutes.

9. With one hand pressing bread down on pan, turn pan over and remove baguette from pan. Place on a serving plate and spread sauce over meat and egg layer.

10. Fold baguette to sandwich meat and egg layer, then slice.

11. Serve with remaining sauce and cucumber slices.

WEIGHTS AND MEASURES

Quantities for this book are given in metric, imperial and American (spoon and cup) measures. Standard spoon and cup measurements used are: 1 teaspoon = 5 ml, 1 tablespoon = 15 ml and 1 cup = 250 ml. All measures are level unless otherwise stated.

LIQUID AND VOLUME MEASURES

Metric	Imperial	American
5 ml	$1/6$ fl oz	1 teaspoon
10 ml	$1/3$ fl oz	1 dessertspoon
15 ml	$1/2$ fl oz	1 tablespoon
60 ml	2 fl oz	$1/4$ cup (4 tablespoons)
85 ml	$2^1/2$ fl oz	$1/3$ cup
90 ml	3 fl oz	$3/8$ cup (6 tablespoons)
125 ml	4 fl oz	$1/2$ cup
180 ml	6 fl oz	$3/4$ cup
250 ml	8 fl oz	1 cup
300 ml	10 fl oz ($1/2$ pint)	$1^1/4$ cups
375 ml	12 fl oz	$1^1/2$ cups
435 ml	14 fl oz	$1^3/4$ cups
500 ml	16 fl oz	2 cups
625 ml	20 fl oz (1 pint)	$2^1/2$ cups
750 ml	24 fl oz ($1^1/5$ pints)	3 cups
1 litre	32 fl oz ($1^3/5$ pints)	4 cups
1.25 litres	40 fl oz (2 pints)	5 cups
1.5 litres	48 fl oz ($2^2/5$ pints)	6 cups
2.5 litres	80 fl oz (4 pints)	10 cups

DRY MEASURES

Metric	Imperial
30 grams	1 ounce
45 grams	$1^1/2$ ounces
55 grams	2 ounces
70 grams	$2^1/2$ ounces
85 grams	3 ounces
100 grams	$3^1/2$ ounces
110 grams	4 ounces
125 grams	$4^1/2$ ounces
140 grams	5 ounces
280 grams	10 ounces
450 grams	16 ounces (1 pound)
500 grams	1 pound, $1^1/2$ ounces
700 grams	$1^1/2$ pounds
800 grams	$1^3/4$ pounds
1 kilogram	2 pounds, 3 ounces
1.5 kilograms	3 pounds, $4^1/2$ ounces
2 kilograms	4 pounds, 6 ounces

OVEN TEMPERATURE

	°C	°F	Gas Regulo
Very slow	120	250	1
Slow	150	300	2
Moderately slow	160	325	3
Moderate	180	350	4
Moderately hot	190/200	370/400	5/6
Hot	210/220	410/440	6/7
Very hot	230	450	8
Super hot	250/290	475/550	9/10

LENGTH

Metric	Imperial
0.5 cm	$1/4$ inch
1 cm	$1/2$ inch
1.5 cm	$3/4$ inch
2.5 cm	1 inch

ABBREVIATION

tsp	teaspoon
Tbsp	tablespoon
g	gram
kg	kilogram
ml	millilitre